ARMIES OF THE PAST

GOING TO WAR IN
ANCIENT GREECE

ARMIES OF THE PAST

GOING TO WAR IN ANCIENT GREECE

Adrian Gilbert

W
FRANKLIN WATTS
LONDON•SYDNEY

✹ ILLUSTRATIONS BY

Mark Bergin
Giovanni Caselli
Chris Molan
Lee Montgomery
Peter Visscher
Maps by Stefan Chabluk

Editor Penny Clarke
Editor-in-Chief John C. Miles

Designer Steve Prosser
Art Director Jonathan Hair

© 2000 Franklin Watts

First published in 2000
by Franklin Watts
96 Leonard Street
London
EC2A 4XD

Franklin Watts Australia
56 O'Riordan Street
Alexandria
NSW 2015

ISBN 0 7496 3811 7

Dewey classification: 938

A CIP catalogue record
for this book is available
from the British Library.

Printed in Hong Kong, China

CONTENTS

ANCIENT GREECE

Labels on map: MACEDONIA, Mt. Olympus, AEGEAN SEA, THESSALY, Thermopylae, BOEOTIA, Chaeronea, Thebes, Leuctra, Plataea, Corinth, Salamis, Piraeus, Athens, Marathon, Argos, PELOPONNESE, MESSENIA, Sparta, LACONIA, PAROS

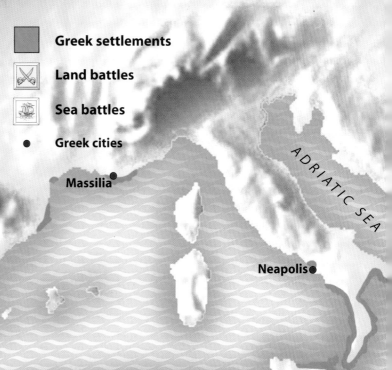

■ Greek settlements

⚔ Land battles

⛵ Sea battles

• Greek cities

Massilia

ADRIATIC SEA

Neapolis

⚔ Syracuse
Syracuse 415BC

THE GREEK WORLD

The civilisation that began to emerge in Greece from about 750BC consisted of many city-states, the inhabitants of which all spoke the Greek language. Some city-states were little more than small towns and their surrounding land, but others, such as Athens and Sparta, became powerful. All had their own armies, and wars were frequent. Due to expanding populations and a shortage of good farmland, many Greeks left their homes to start up settlements in other lands.

Kinyps

TRIPOLIS

Late 8th-century BC armour from Argos, the earliest complete Greek armour

Origins 1200BC
The early Greek Mycenaean civilisation is overthrown. Greece enters a 'dark age' until around 750BC when a new Greek culture emerges.

City-states 750-650BC
Rival Greek-speaking city-states emerge. Each has its own army.

Persian invasions 490-479BC
Greece is invaded by Persia in 490BC and again in 480BC. On both occasions the Greeks defeat the Persians and force them to withdraw.

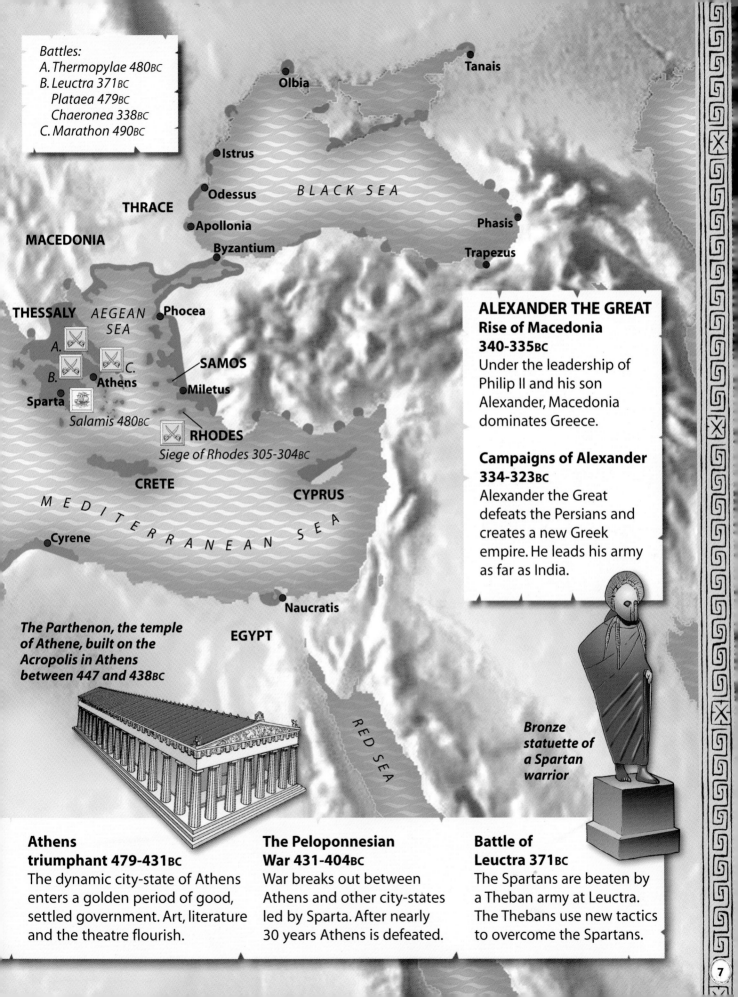

Battles:
A. Thermopylae 480BC
B. Leuctra 371BC
   Plataea 479BC
   Chaeronea 338BC
C. Marathon 490BC

Tanais

Olbia

Istrus

BLACK SEA

Odessus

THRACE

Apollonia

Phasis

MACEDONIA

Byzantium

Trapezus

THESSALY   AEGEAN
           SEA   Phocea

A.

SAMOS

B.   Athens

C.

Sparta   Miletus

Salamis 480BC

RHODES
Siege of Rhodes 305-304BC

CRETE   CYPRUS

M E D I T E R R A N E A N   S E A

Cyrene

ALEXANDER THE GREAT
Rise of Macedonia 340-335BC
Under the leadership of Philip II and his son Alexander, Macedonia dominates Greece.

Campaigns of Alexander 334-323BC
Alexander the Great defeats the Persians and creates a new Greek empire. He leads his army as far as India.

Naucratis

EGYPT

The Parthenon, the temple of Athene, built on the Acropolis in Athens between 447 and 438BC

R E D   S E A

Bronze statuette of a Spartan warrior

Athens triumphant 479-431BC
The dynamic city-state of Athens enters a golden period of good, settled government. Art, literature and the theatre flourish.

The Peloponnesian War 431-404BC
War breaks out between Athens and other city-states led by Sparta. After nearly 30 years Athens is defeated.

Battle of Leuctra 371BC
The Spartans are beaten by a Theban army at Leuctra. The Thebans use new tactics to overcome the Spartans.

Soldiers of the City-State

Greek city-states adopted similar ways of waging war. Around the 7th century BC cavalry, which had been an important part of earlier Greek armies, was replaced by heavily armed infantry called *hoplites*.

At the height of its power Athens, the largest of the city-states, had a huge army. The Athenians elected ten generals (*strategoi*) who helped govern the state in peacetime and lead the army in war. If a general displeased the people he could be sacked and punished.

WARFARE AND FARMING

In ancient Greece warfare and agriculture were closely linked. Military campaigns usually did not last long so that soldiers could return to their farms at harvest time.

Military writers believed that good farmers made good warriors. On becoming a soldier, a hoplite swore an oath to defend 'the wheat, the barley, the vines, the olives and the figs'.

Greek hoplites preparing for war

PREPARING FOR WAR

In time of war, all male citizens of Athens over the age of 17 were required to serve as soldiers. Hoplites were mainly recruited from small farmers. These men were wealthy enough to supply their own armour and weapons.

FAMOUS COMMANDERS

PERICLES (495-429BC)
A great statesman and general, Pericles played a major role in the expansion of Athenian power in the 5th century BC. He supervised the rebuilding of the Acropolis.

ALEXANDER THE GREAT (356-323BC)
A supremely gifted soldier, Alexander united the Greeks under his command. In less than a decade he conquered the Persian empire.

Unlike the elected generals of Athens, Alexander had total power over his army and was ruthless in imposing his will.

MILITIADES (550-489BC)
Militiades defeated the Persians at the battle of Marathon (490BC). But after failing to capture the island of Paros, he returned to Athens in disgrace and was fined.

PEPIKΛHΣ

WARRIORS ALL
Greeks from all occupations regarded military service as a great honour. Although he was short and pot-bellied, the philosopher Socrates (469-399BC) fought with great bravery as a hoplite.

The playwright Sophocles (496-406BC) was a distinguished naval commander, while the author and dramatist Aeschylus (525-456BC) fought the Persians at Marathon, where his brother was killed.

THE PRICE OF COMMAND
Athenian generals could find themselves harshly treated by their own people. After the naval battle of Arginusae in 406BC, eight commanders were sentenced to death because they had not rescued Athenian sailors who had fallen in the water.

Socrates tried to stop the sentence being carried out, but all eight were executed by the vengeful citizens.

Socrates 469-399BC

SPARTA

The Spartans were a Greek people who lived in the Peloponnese (the southernmost part of Greece). In the 8th century BC they conquered the neighbouring state of Messenia, enslaving its people. A series of wars with Argos and a revolt by the Messenians in 630BC led Sparta to develop a unique military society to protect its territory.

Only Spartan-born males could become citizens, and all had to join the army. They were not allowed to do any other work, and spent all their time training for war. Sparta had two kings who acted as generals in war, although real power lay in the hands of the five *ephors* (magistrates).

The Spartans were the most feared warriors in Greece. The writer and philosopher Plutarch noted that they:

'Marched in step to the pipe, leaving no confusion in their hearts, but calmly and cheerfully advanced into danger.'

SPARTAN TROOPS

Spartan soldiers were equipped with armour and weapons in the same way as the soldiers of other Greek armies, although their red tunics and cloaks made them stand out on the battlefield.

Spartan soldiers were also distinguished by their long hair, which they carefully combed before battle.

THE WAY OF THE WARRIOR

All Spartan men had to live in barracks with their fellow soldiers until old age. They were not allowed to marry until the age of 30, and even then a soldier was only allowed to visit his wife and family at intervals.

Other city-states both respected and feared the Spartans' bravery and fighting skills.

A Spartan soldier ready for battle wears his red cloak and bronze cuirass (torso armour)

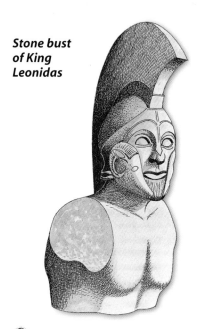

Stone bust of King Leonidas

RESISTANCE

As Spartans, it was unthinkable for Leonidas and his men to flee before the relentless onslaught of the Persians at Thermopylae. However, their brave stand was not wasted as it encouraged the other Greek city-states to fight and finally defeat the Persians.

After Thermopylae, the invaders marched south and captured Athens, but were defeated at the naval battle of Salamis. The following year, 479BC, the Persians were decisively beaten on land at the battle of Plataea and were driven from Greece.

THE PERSIAN INVASION

In 480BC a vast Persian army commanded by the emperor Xerxes invaded Greece. A small force of Spartans led by King Leonidas was annihilated while trying to defend a mountainous pass at Thermopylae.

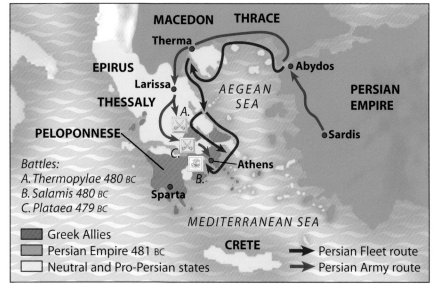

Battles:
A. Thermopylae 480 BC
B. Salamis 480 BC
C. Plataea 479 BC

- Greek Allies
- Persian Empire 481 BC
- Neutral and Pro-Persian states
→ Persian Fleet route
→ Persian Army route

HARD LIVES

SPARTAN GIRLS

Spartan girls, unlike those in the rest of Greece, were encouraged to take physical exercise and compete in athletic events.

It was hoped that this would make them fitter and stronger mothers, who would give birth to more and healthier children.

SPARTAN BOYS

At the age of seven, boys were taken from their mothers and sent to schools which emphasised discipline and exercise. Conditions were harsh to prepare them for war.

HELOTS

The people captured by the Spartans were called helots. They worked as slaves, farming the land. The Spartans were always fearful of helot rebellion, and during peacetime the army kept the helots in order.

THE HOPLITE

Bronze helmet

Horsehair plume

Linen tunic

Stiffened linen cuirass

Sword

Argive shield

Leather apron

Bronze greaves

Spear

Sandals

Butt spike

Hoplites became the main defenders of the city-state, and over time forced the aristocrats to give them a share of power in what became citizen-democracies. As a result, they had an important say in deciding when and how wars should be fought. In battle, hoplites fought shoulder-to-shoulder in a tightly packed formation called a *phalanx*. Phalanx warfare was extremely effective as long as the hoplites held their positions and worked together.

According to Archilochus, the 7th-century BC poet, a good hoplite was 'a short man firmly placed upon his legs, with a courageous heart, not to be uprooted from the spot where he plants his feet'.

WEAPONS AND ARMOUR
Besides his large 'argive' shield, the hoplite was protected by a bronze helmet and a cuirass. To protect the lower part of his legs he wore greaves, which were made of thin bronze and clipped around his calves.

A leather apron was sometimes attached to the shield to give extra protection to the leg area. His weapons were a thrusting spear and a sword.

WEAPONS

SHIELDS
Hoplite shields were a symbol of courage, and to throw one away in battle was a disgrace. Spartan women told their soldiers to return either with their shields or on them.

SWORDS
Hoplites only used their short iron swords if their spears were broken or for fighting at close quarters.

Hoplite sword

Hoplite spear

SPEARS
Spears were the hoplite's principal weapon. The shaft was made from a strong wood such as ash, and besides the iron spearhead it had a bronze butt spike. This was used to stab men who had fallen to the ground during the battle.

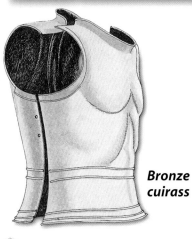

Bronze cuirass

ARMOUR
The cuirass, which protected the chest and back, was made up of two plates that were joined together at the sides. Heavy bronze cuirasses (often shaped with the muscles of the torso) were popular among hoplite officers, although leather and stiffened linen were also common.

Shields were made from thick strips of oak, covered with leather or bronze.

A HEAVY BURDEN
The weapons and armour carried and worn by the hoplites were very heavy. The 6-millimetre thick cuirass could weigh up to 13.5 kilos and the shield added another 9 kilos.

Overall, the hoplite's armour amounted to about half his body weight. As a result, hoplites could not move very fast and tended to favour simple defensive tactics.

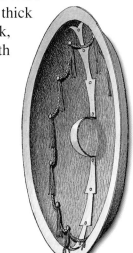

Back of a hoplite's shield showing holding straps

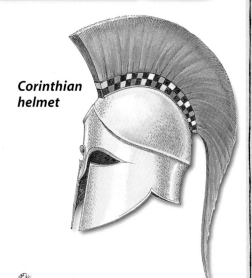

Corinthian helmet

HELMET DESIGN
The Corinthian helmet, which covered much of the wearer's face, was very popular in the 6th and 5th centuries BC. It was very heavy, but provided excellent protection.

An elaborate horsehair crest was attached to the crown of the helmet as a means of identification – and to make its wearer look more impressive.

CAVALRY AND SKIRMISHERS

The packed phalanx of hoplites dominated Greek warfare for more than 200 years, but during the 5th century BC – as a result of the Persian Wars (490-479BC) and the Peloponnesian War (431-404BC) – tactics began to change, and cavalry became important.

The phalanx was effective on flat, open ground but not in hills and rough country, areas which suited lightly armed troops. Cavalry went on scouting missions and hunted down fleeing enemy infantrymen, while skirmishers (lightly armed foot soldiers) harassed the enemy's phalanx before the main battle.

The Athenian commander Iphicrates believed that armies would be more effective if cavalry and light troops fought alongside the hoplite phalanx:

'The light-armed troops are like the hands, the cavalry like the feet, the line of men-at-arms like chest and breastplate, and the general like the head.'

CAVALRY

Cavalrymen normally came from wealthy families because buying and keeping horses was an expensive business.

The best cavalry came from the northern Greek state of Thessaly. For centuries, the grazing land for which the state was famous had led to the breeding of fine horses and a tradition of outstanding horsemanship had developed.

WEAPONS

Cavalrymen rode their horses without stirrups and usually bareback. They rarely wore armour and their weapons consisted of a couple of javelins and a sword.

When fighting against hoplites, cavalry threw their javelins at the enemy soldiers and then retreated to safety. They were not expected to take on the phalanx in hand-to-hand combat.

Lightly armed cavalryman

LIGHT TROOPS

Psiloi and *gymnets* were two groups of lightly armed Greek skirmishers. In addition there were the *peltasts* who were recruited from Thrace and harried the enemy phalanx.

The Athenians used Scythian archers, although the best bowmen came from Crete. The island of Rhodes was famous as a source of slingers.

PSILOI
These troops wielded a club and threw stones to harass the enemy.

GYMNETS
Equipped only with swords, gymnets were of little use in a major phalanx battle.

ARCHERS
Archers with powerful bows provided long-range firepower to support the phalanx.

SLINGERS
Slingers fired stones at the enemy with considerable accuracy.

PELTASTS
Thracian peltasts were armed with javelins and carried a crescent-shaped shield.

SLINGSHOTS AND BOWS

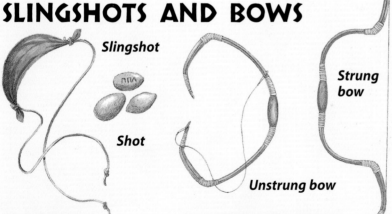

Slingshot

Shot

Strung bow

Unstrung bow

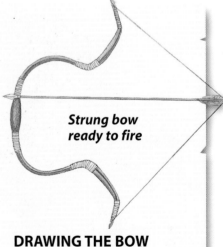

Strung bow ready to fire

SLINGSHOTS
Shot was made from small stones, clay or lead and hurled from a leather sling. Sometimes the slinger inscribed messages on to his shot, such as 'Take that!'

COMPOSITE BOWS
Composite bows, which were made from a combination of wood, horn, bone and animal sinews, were strong and could fire arrows a long way with great accuracy.

DRAWING THE BOW
The most powerful composite bows – used by Scythian archers – were very difficult to draw back, so archers had to be extremely strong.

THE SHOCK OF BATTLE

Early Greek civilisations had fought each other in small groups, but from around 750BC onwards city-states began to organise their soldiers to fight in phalanxes. Battles in which one phalanx fought another became the standard form of confrontation in Greek warfare over the next four centuries.

The two sides would normally agree on the site of a battle by picking a flat piece of land on which the phalanx could move easily. After sacrifices to the gods, the two armies lined up facing each other. Then the order to attack would be given, and the two great masses of shields and spears crashed into each other.

BOEOTIA
Leuctra ● ●Thebes
Battle of Leuctra 371BC ●Athens
PELOPONNESE
MESSENIA
●Sparta
LACONIA MEDITERRANEAN
SEA

BATTLE OF LEUCTRA
In 371BC Epaminondas's Theban army defeated a more powerful Spartan force using new tactics. The enemy's right wing was overwhelmed and the Spartan king and all his best troops were killed.

BATTLE TACTICS

PHALANX AT WORK
The phalanx could be several hundred men across and usually anything from eight to 16 men deep. The first three ranks stabbed at their opponents with their spears. Ranks behind tried to push them forward to break the enemy line.

Spartans

Thebans

THEBAN TACTICS
At Leuctra, Thebans used large numbers of light troops and massed their hoplites into a 50-deep phalanx on their left wing, while their centre and right wing hung back. The 12-deep Spartan phalanx could not withstand the Thebans' charge.

INTERLOCKING SHIELDS
Within the phalanx, each hoplite's shield partly protected him and the man on his left. In battle, the phalanx tended to move to the right as each man sought protection from his neighbour's shield.

🏛 CLASH OF SHIELDS

Success in a typical hoplite battle depended upon raw courage and brute strength. Once the two sides were locked in battle, the side that pushed forward and broke into the enemy phalanx won the battle. Each hoplite tried to stab the vulnerable and unprotected parts of his opponents while trying to protect himself with his own shield. Hoplites who fell during the fighting were trampled underfoot and stabbed with swords or the butt spikes on the spears of their enemies. The fighting was bloody, vicious and terrifying.

Greek musician playing the auloi

🏛 MARCHING TO MUSIC

The phalanx was accompanied by musicians playing horns and double-piped instruments called *auloi*. While the music encouraged the hoplites to fight (and frightened the enemy), it also helped the soldiers keep in step as they marched. Keeping in step was important in the closely packed phalanx formation.

Combat between phalanxes was a very bloody business. The Greek soldier and historian Xenophon described the battlefield after the second Battle of Coronea in 394BC:

'The earth was stained in blood, and the remains of friends and enemies lay side-by-side. There were shattered shields, broken spears and unsheathed swords, some lying about on the ground, others stuck in corpses, and others still gripped as if to strike even in death.'

SIEGE WARFARE

Until the Peloponnesian War (431-404BC), the Greeks had rarely besieged each others' cities. Battles were fought in the open – protected by their walls, cities were normally safe, unless defeated by starvation or treachery.

Among the changes that took place in Greek warfare in the 5th century BC were the development of siege weapons and special techniques to break down city walls. Sieges became more common; defenders increased the strength of city walls and attackers invented more powerful siege weapons.

SIEGE IN PROGRESS

Breaking down the city's walls became the key objective of a besieging army (below). Tunnellers burrowed to undermine foundations and battering rams smashed their way through at weak points.

Siege artillery – crossbows and catapults – fired missiles, while archers shot at enemy troops manning the walls. Later, armoured siege towers might be trundled into place to allow the attackers to get over the walls and enter the city.

Siege tower

Battering ram

THE THEORY OF SIEGES

During the 4th century BC many military writers produced manuals about siege warfare. Dionysius I of Syracuse (in Sicily) used the latest siege engines – including catapults and towers – during his successful assault on Moyta in 397BC. His ideas influenced the Macedonians, who became masters of siege warfare under Philip II and Alexander.

SIEGE WEAPONS

Catapult

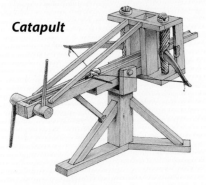

CATAPULT

This type of stone-firing catapult was used by Alexander at the siege of Tyre (332BC). Each arm of the catapult was held in place by tightly twisted sinew or horse hair, which provided the power to fire the projectile.

CROSSBOW

Siege crossbows operated like an ordinary bow, but because the bow was so large and stiff, the string had to be pulled back using a winch. Crossbows were also used by soldiers on the city walls to fire at siege equipment such as battering rams and siege towers.

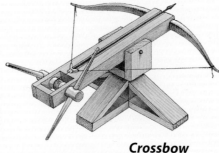

Crossbow

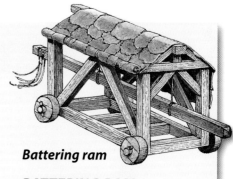

Battering ram

BATTERING RAM

A battering ram consisted of a tree trunk with a metal point fitted to one end suspended from a wheeled frame. When swung, the ram smashed through weak points in the walls. The soldiers operating the ram were protected from enemy arrows by the hide-covered roof and sides.

PELOPONNESIAN WAR

The rivalry between Athens and Sparta and their many allies burst into open warfare in 431BC. The turning point of the war was the Athenians' siege of Syracuse in 415BC (below).

Helped by the Spartans, the garrison of Syracuse held out, defeating first the Athenian navy and then destroying their army.

THE CITY-TAKER

During the siege of Rhodes in 305-304BC, the attackers constructed an enormous siege tower. Protected by iron plates, it was called the *helepolis*, or city-taker (right).

The tower, which is thought to have been 42 metres high, had catapults inside it. Fortunately for the people of Rhodes, the tower eventually proved ineffective.

Wheels rolled tower forwards

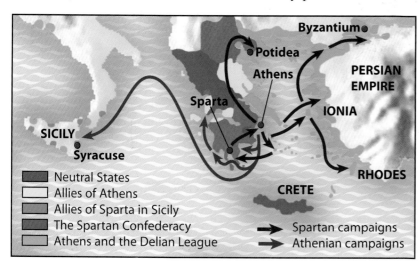

- Neutral States
- Allies of Athens
- Allies of Sparta in Sicily
- The Spartan Confederacy
- Athens and the Delian League

→ Spartan campaigns
→ Athenian campaigns

Byzantium
Potidea
Athens
PERSIAN EMPIRE
Sparta
IONIA
SICILY
Syracuse
RHODES
CRETE

WAR AT SEA

Greek shipbuilding was influenced by the Phoenicians, a seafaring people who lived around the eastern and southern shores of the Mediterranean.

The first Greek warships, or *penteconters*, had 50 oarsmen seated in a row. In the 8th century BC the Greeks copied the Phoenicians' *bireme*, with two rows of oars. This developed into the *trireme* (three rows of oars) in the 5th century. Later, even larger ships were built.

MARITIME ATHENS

Athens had a long history of sea trade, and after the battle of Salamis (480BC) it built up a powerful navy. This helped Athens acquire a large empire in and around the Aegean Sea, although this caused much resentment among other Greek city-states.

The Athenian navy was very expensive and needed large numbers of rowers – over 20,000 men on one occasion. Rowers were recruited from free men who could not afford to buy the armour and weapons needed by hoplites.

Large single sail

Banks of rowers

THE TRIREME

Triremes (above) were about 40 metres long and had a crew of around 200: 170 rowers and 30 crewmen and marines. Triremes usually sailed within sight of land; in the evenings the ships were beached and the crew spent the night on shore.

Before a battle the sails and rigging were taken down and the trireme was propelled entirely by its rowers.

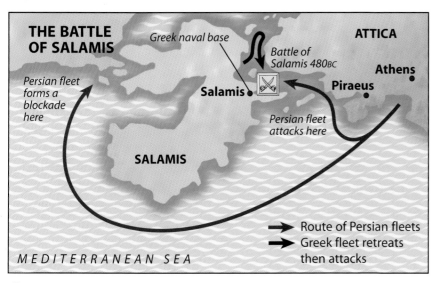

THE BATTLE OF SALAMIS

Greek naval base

ATTICA

Battle of Salamis 480BC

Athens

Piraeus

Salamis

Persian fleet forms a blockade here

Persian fleet attacks here

SALAMIS

→ Route of Persian fleets
→ Greek fleet retreats then attacks

MEDITERRANEAN SEA

BATTLE OF SALAMIS 480BC

During the second Persian invasion, a fleet of 200 Greek triremes faced 800 Persian ships. The Greeks withdrew to the narrow channels around the island of Salamis so the Persians had no room to manoeuvre.

When the Greeks attacked, their fighting and rowing skills forced the Persians to retreat. After this defeat, the Persians began to withdraw from Greece.

BRONZE RAM

The prow, or front, of the trireme was made of bronze and rammed enemy ships. The rowers propelled the trireme fast enough for the ram to hole the enemy's hull.

Many Greek ships had an eye painted near the prow to ward off the 'evil eye' – a motif that is still sometimes seen on Greek boats today.

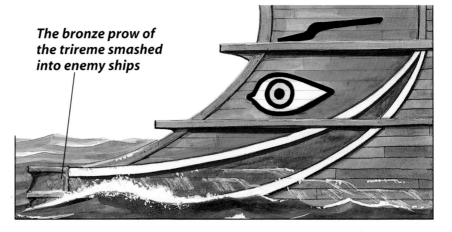

The bronze prow of the trireme smashed into enemy ships

BATTLE TACTICS

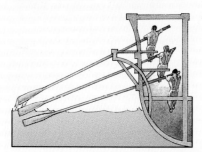

RAM AHEAD
The usual tactic was for the attacking ship to ram the enemy vessel amidships. If this was successful, the enemy ship would be so badly damaged that it would sink in a matter of minutes.

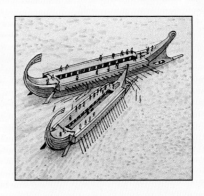

ROWING A TRIREME
Oars were arranged in three rows with a man to each oar. For short periods the rowers could propel their trireme through the water at speeds of up to 16 km/h – incredibly fast for human power alone.

ATTACK FROM THE SIDE
A complex tactic was that in which a trireme went alongside an enemy ship, pulling in its own oars as it did so and smashing those of the enemy. The disabled ship was now vulnerable to boarding or ramming.

AN ARMY ON THE MOVE

Hoplite armies always needed large numbers of civilians to help transport soldiers' weapons and gear. As well as servants and slaves on foot carrying baggage, mules, horses and carts moved heavier equipment.

While on the march, hoplites normally ate barley, which was ground up and mixed into a porridge. If food was plentiful they might eat cheese, salted meat and onions. And at certain times of the year they would be able to scavenge local produce, such as figs and olives.

PREPARING THE WAY

In the Spartan army, men who had been rejected as not good enough to become hoplites were used to clear the way for the baggage carts and other heavy equipment.

They were given shovels, axes and sickles, and they played an important role in making sure the army could move to the battlefield with as little delay as possible.

Cavalry trooper

Packhorse

Servant

Foot soldier

CAMP FOLLOWERS

When an army went on a long campaign, it took with it craftsmen to help repair arms and equipment damaged in battle or in transit.

These included blacksmiths, carpenters and leather workers. Other civilians, or camp followers, included the hoplites' servants, women and even children. Sometimes so many camp followers accompanied the army that it became very slow and cumbersome. Commanders tried to limit the number of camp followers, but seldom with much success.

🏛 BATTLE PREPARATIONS

Getting ready for battle was an elaborate business for a hoplite. This is shown on the left in this vase painting. He combed and tidied his hair before putting on the heavy Corinthian helmet. The cuirass came next, followed by the greaves on his legs.

Putting on his armour properly was important, as every hoplite knew that in a few hours he might either be a victor, or among the vanquished dead.

Vase painting (500BC) of hoplites arming for battle

🏛 SERVANTS AND SLAVES

Each Spartan hoplite had a helot to carry his weapons and armour. An Athenian hoplite used one of the slaves or servants who worked on his farm.

Slaves and servants also prepared food and built shelters. Before battle, they cleaned and prepared their masters' weapons. Great care was taken of shields, which had an almost religious importance for the warriors.

A servant packs a shield in its leather cover

🏛 MEDICAL AID

Although the Greeks had only very limited knowledge of how the body worked, attempts were made to help wounded and injured men. Philip II employed surgeons in his army and they operated on soldiers injured in battle. There were no anaesthetics. If his wounds became infected a soldier would almost certainly die.

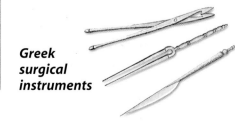

Greek surgical instruments

WAR AND THE GODS

The Greeks worshipped many gods and believed that they must have their approval if they were to be successful in battle. And yet, while the Greeks thought that wars were inevitable, they did not always consider them to be a good thing.

Many writers described the damage and suffering caused by conflicts. The Theban poet Pindar warned that war 'was a sweet thing to him that does not know it, but to him who has made a trial of it, it is a thing of fear'.

 SACRIFICE

Before battle, a commander would order the sacrifice of a goat or a sheep. It was hoped that the sacrifice would please the gods and bring victory.

GODS

ARES

The god of war, Ares, was violent and short-tempered. According to the poet Homer, Zeus said: 'To me you are the most hateful of all the gods who hold Olympus.'

ATHENE

Athene, the patron of Athens, was also the goddess of wisdom and war. She was often shown wearing hoplite armour and carrying weapons.

NIKE

'Nike' was the Greek word for victory, and was usually personified as a beautiful winged goddess, sometimes carrying a spear and a shield. Statues of Nike were common throughout Greece.

SOPHOCLES

As well as being a great playwright, Sophocles (*c*.496-406BC) was a naval commander who played a leading role in the capture of Samos. Like many other Greek writers and artists, he had practical experience of war and wrote about it in his plays.

A victorious hoplite - bound by the nomima

PRISONERS

Until the Peloponnesian War (431-404BC) the city-states would normally swap their prisoners after a battle. But the old rules of war were largely ignored in this brutal conflict, and prisoners were often slaughtered by their captors.

At the end of one battle during the war, Philocles, the victorious Athenian admiral, ordered that the crews from two captured triremes should be thrown off a cliff.

A Spartan hoplite prepares to kill a prisoner

RULES OF WAR

The hoplite (left) represented what was best in the city-state: an honest farmer brave in battle and generous in victory. He was theoretically bound by the rules of war called the *nomima*. This included fair treatment of prisoners.

THE ARMY OF MACEDONIA

The northern state of Macedonia played little part in Greek affairs until Philip II became king in 359BC. He built up a strong army and began to expand his territories by conquest, first to the east and then south towards the Greek heartland.

The other Greek city-states opposed Macedonian expansion, but they did not band together to fight Philip until it was too late. In 338BC, at the battle of Chaeronea, the forces of the city-states were decisively defeated and Philip became master of Greece.

Macedonian pikemen advancing in a phalanx were an awesome sight. One writer explained how Aemilius Paulus, a Roman commander who fought the Macedonians, remembered his fear on seeing the enemy:

'He considered the formidable appearance of their front, bristling with arms, and was taken with fear and alarm: nothing he had ever seen before was its equal.'

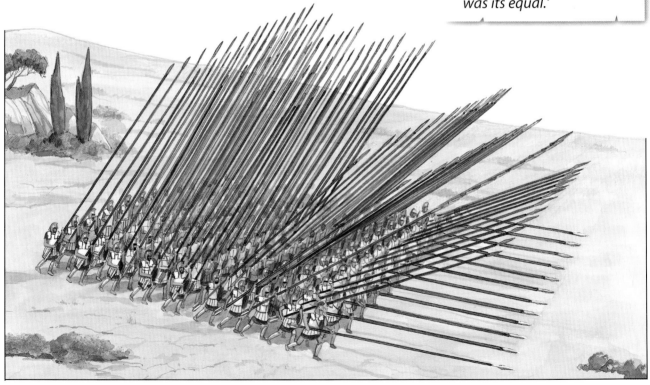

THE MACEDONIAN PHALANX

Unlike the Greek phalanx, which depended on soldiers forming a defensive wall, the Macedonian phalanx relied on offence to defeat the enemy (above). Armour was lighter and the soldiers' *sarissa* (spear) much longer. This meant that from the first five ranks of the Macedonian phalanx, spear points projected at the enemy.

PHILIP'S ARMY

The phalanx was central to the success of the Macedonian army, but Philip also used lightly armed troops. He introduced a new type of infantry called *hypaspists*. Armed with swords and short spears they protected the flanks of the phalanx. Unlike the Greek city-states, Macedonia was ruled by a king with his aristocratic followers (called Companions), most of whom fought as mounted soldiers. As a result, cavalry was very important in the Macedonian army.

The phalangite's spear was up to 6 m in length.

THE PHALANGITE

The soldiers of the Macedonian phalanx were called *phalangites*. They were lightly equipped with a simple helmet and light armour, and because they needed both hands to hold the sarissa, they wore their small shield slung over their shoulder by a leather strap. The phalangites were highly disciplined and underwent rugged training involving long marches carrying their equipment.

MACEDONIA

Ivory carving of Philip II

PHILIP II

Philip (*c*.382-336BC) was a fine trainer of soldiers and a skilful general who combined light and heavy infantry with cavalry to outmanoeuvre his slower opponents.

NEW HELMETS

The Macedonian army used different helmets to those worn by Athenian hoplites in the 5th century and earlier. The Thracian helmet covered less of the wearer's face, enabling him to see and hear better during a battle.

Thracian helmet

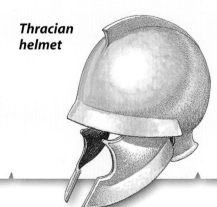

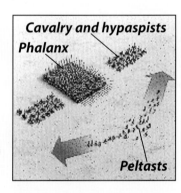

Cavalry and hypaspists
Phalanx
Peltasts

MACEDONIAN TACTICS

Peltasts and other light troops would soften up the enemy with missile attacks. They would then retire behind the main phalanx, which was supported on the flanks by cavalry and hypaspists.

ALEXANDER THE GREAT

Alexander the Great benefited from inheriting the combined Macedonian/Greek army built up by his father Philip, and used it to go campaigning in the east.

Intensely ambitious, Alexander always tried to destroy an enemy army as a first step to seizing new territory. Once the Persian empire had been overthrown, he incorporated Persian troops in his army to allow him to continue his advance. Only the refusal of Alexander's soldiers to follow him into India halted his career of conquest.

COMPANIONS

The eight squadrons of mounted troops known as the Companions were the elite troops of Alexander's army. They were recruited from the Macedonian aristocracy.

The Companions were more heavily equipped than traditional Greek cavalry and carried a long thrusting spear. They did not skirmish before the main infantry battle but, arranged in a wedge-shaped formation, charged directly at the enemy.

Bust of Alexander the Great

One of Alexander's Companions

ALEXANDER

Succeeding to the throne in 336BC, the 20-year-old Alexander (above) immediately began an invasion of the Persian empire.

Over the next 13 years he engaged in almost constant warfare, dying of exhaustion and fever in Babylon in 323BC. Although brave, Alexander could also be very cruel, killing anyone who displeased him.

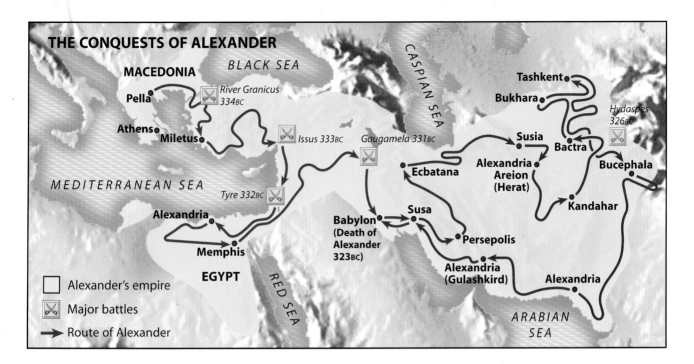

THE CONQUESTS OF ALEXANDER

MACEDONIA
BLACK SEA
CASPIAN SEA
Pella
River Granicus 334BC
Tashkent
Bukhara
Hydaspes 326BC
Athens
Miletus
Issus 333BC
Gaugamela 331BC
Susia
Bactra
Bucephala
MEDITERRANEAN SEA
Ecbatana
Alexandria Areion (Herat)
Tyre 332BC
Alexandria
Susa
Babylon (Death of Alexander 323BC)
Persepolis
Kandahar
Memphis
EGYPT
Alexandria (Gulashkird)
Alexandria
RED SEA
ARABIAN SEA

☐ Alexander's empire
⚔ Major battles
➔ Route of Alexander

ALEXANDER'S EMPIRE

Alexander defeated the Persians in Asia Minor at Granicus and Issus before conquering Egypt. He then led his forces into Persia, destroying the Persian army at Gaugamela. Although he defeated an Indian army at Hydaspes, his exhausted troops refused to go further, forcing Alexander to return to Persia.

Alexander was a brilliant speaker, inspiring his troops to fight harder in battle. This is part of his speech to the army before the Battle of Issus (333BC):

'We Macedonians are to fight Medes and Persians, nations long steeped in luxury, while we have long been hardened by warlike toils and dangers; and above all it will be a fight of free men against slaves.'

ELEPHANTS

At the battle of Hydaspes, Alexander saw elephants for the first time. He then began using them in his own armies, adding fighting 'castles' for archers and spearmen.

After Alexander's death, elephants were widely used by the Greek generals who succeeded him – many were brought back from India to Greece.

Greek war elephant ready for battle

GLOSSARY

Dates in ancient Greece are dated backwards from the birth of Christ (BC). Centuries are listed below.

First century = 1-99BC
Second century = 100-199BC
Third century = 200-299BC
Fourth century = 300-399BC
Fifth century = 400-499BC
Sixth century = 500-599BC
Seventh century = 600-699BC

Piper playing the auloi

Argive shield
Round concave shield used by hoplites.

Aristocratic
People of the highest class who belonged to the powerful land-owning families. From the Greek word *aristoi*, 'the best people'.

Auloi
The double pipes that accompanied soldiers into battle. They were fitted with reeds and are thought to have made a sound a little like the modern oboe.

Campaign
The period when an army marched away to fight an enemy.

Citizen
A free male person within the city-state. He was given the right to vote but was also expected to fight if the state became involved in a war.

Cuirass
Armour consisting of a breastplate and backplate to protect the soldier's torso. The cuirass could be made from a variety of materials, including bronze, leather and stiffened linen.

Democracy
The political system that operated in many Greek city-states, especially Athens. In democratic states, citizens were given a say in how the city was run. This included the right to vote.

Helots
People captured by the Spartans who were treated like slaves. They were forced to work on Sparta's farms so Spartan men could concentrate on training to become soldiers.

Hoplite
Heavily armoured Greek foot soldier. The name is thought to derive from the word *hopla*, meaning the weapons and equipment that had to be carried by the soldier.

Bust of Pericles

Hypaspist
Soldier in the Macedonian army who was more lightly armed and equipped than the hoplite, and who fought between the cavalry and the phalangites of the main phalanx. The word means 'shield bearer'.

Javelin
Short spear mainly used for throwing at the enemy.

Marine
Soldier who operated on board a ship, and was trained in ship-to-ship fighting.

Nomima
Code of conduct that encouraged soldiers to treat others fairly, especially prisoners.

Non-combatant
Person involved in a war who was not a soldier. This included people such as musicians and surgeons.

Peloponnese
The southernmost part of Greece, linked to the rest of the country by the strip of land known as the Isthmus of Corinth. The area was inhabited by the Dorian tribes and included the city-states of Sparta and Corinth.

Peltast
Lightly armed soldier, originating from the northern state of Thrace. Peltasts became common in Greek armies from the end of the 5th century onwards. The name is derived from the word *pelte*, referring to the distinctive curved shields carried by Thracian peltasts.

Phalangite
Macedonian soldier who wore little armour but was armed with a long spear (*sarissa*) and fought within the phalanx.

Phalanx
Tightly packed formation of infantrymen armed with spears, made up of either hoplites or Macedonian phalangites. The phalanx was typically anything from eight to 16 ranks deep, although the Thebans sometimes deployed a phalanx that was up to 50 ranks deep.

Skirmishing
Form of fighting by lightly armed and equipped soldiers, operating individually in the open.

The helepolis: the Greeks' iron-clad siege tower

INDEX

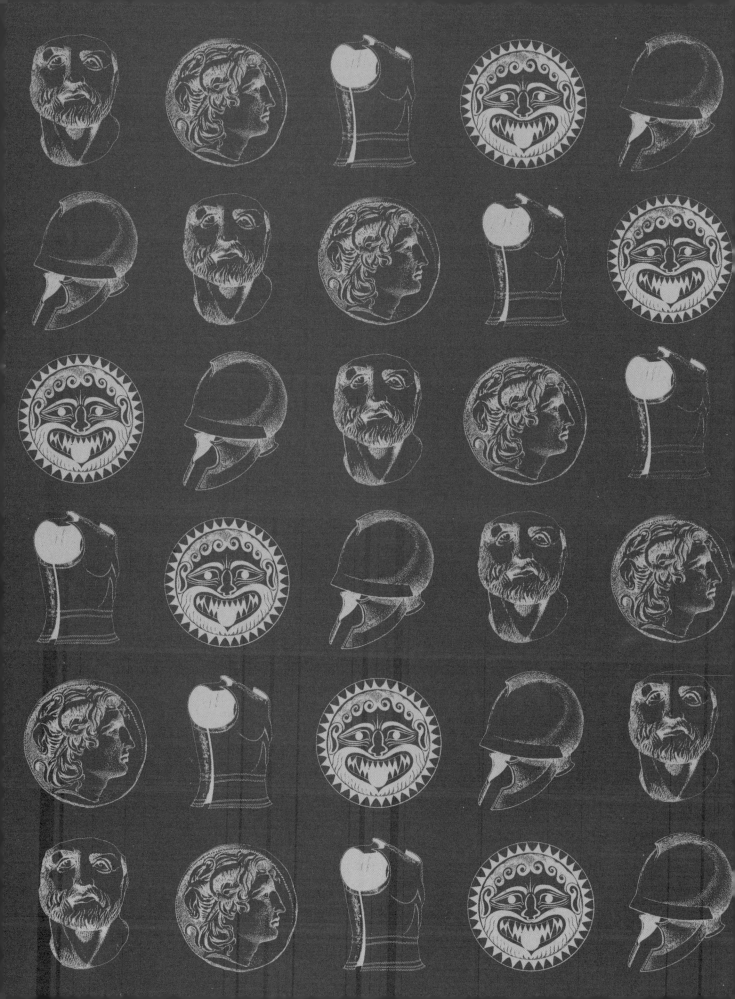